GET READY FOR GRADE 1

Time and Money

Penny Dowdy

QEB

QEB Publishing

Editor: Amanda Askew
Designer: Red Paper Design
Illustrator: Bill Bolton

Contents

Time to the **Hour**

When the big hands point to the 12, a new hour starts. Look at the clock:

The big hand points to the 12.
The little hand points to the 3.
It is 3 o'clock. You can also write 3:00.

What time is it? Write each answer in the blank.

__ o'clock or __:____

__ o'clock or __:____

__ o'clock or __:____

Read the time. Draw the hands on each clock.

11:00

8:00

6:00

3:00

10:00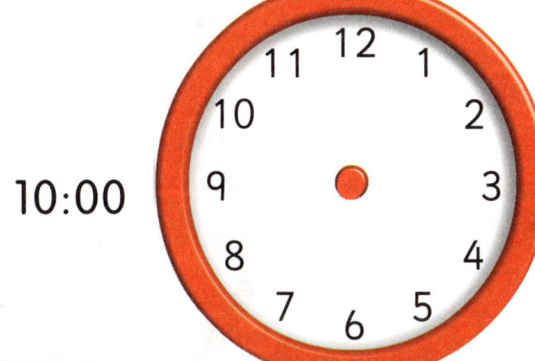

5:00

Note: Point out that the big hand touches the numbers. The little hand does not.

Time to the Half Hour

When the big hand points to the 6, half of an hour has passed. Look at the clock:

The big hand points to the 6.
The little hand is between the 1 and the 2.
It is half past 1. You can also write 1:30.

What time is it? Write each answer in the blank.

Half past __ or __:____

Half past __ or __:____

Half past __ or __:____

1:30

10:30

8:30

5:30

12:30

7:30

Note: As the time is between two hours, the hour hand is halfway to the next hour.

Clocks

Some clocks have faces. These clocks have hands to show the time.

Some clocks do not have faces. These clocks have numbers to show the time.

Match the clocks that tell the same time.

8:30   7:30

4:00   9:00

Kim wakes up at:

Jason wakes up at:

Carlos eats breakfast at:

Nikki eats breakfast at:

Betty has recess at:

Darren has recess at:

Jin eats dinner at:

Mia eats dinner at:

Clare goes to bed at:

Tina goes to bed at:

Note: Teach children to read both digital and analog clocks.

Time of **Day**

You do things at certain times of day.

Morning is the time when the sun comes up.
It ends at noon, or lunch time.

Afternoon is the time after morning until
the sun starts to set.

Night is the time when the sun goes down.
It lasts until the sun comes up again!

Cross out each wrong answer.

You eat 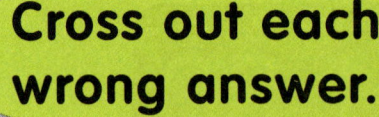   in the morning.
at night.

You eat    in the afternoon.
in the morning.

You eat    in the morning.
at night.

Check the correct box to show what time of day each activity would be done.

morning ☐

afternoon ☐

night ☐

morning ☐

afternoon ☐

night ☐

morning ☐

afternoon ☐

night ☐

Note: Have children make a list of things they do during each part of the day.

11

How Long?

We have names for different lengths of time.

A second is very fast. For example, it only takes a second to say the word "banana."

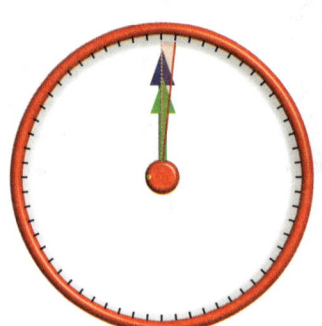

A minute is longer. A minute is 60 seconds. A song lasts for a few minutes.

An hour is much longer. An hour is 60 minutes. Movies can last an hour or more.

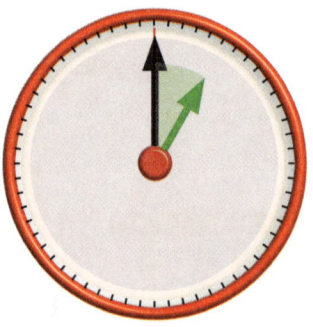

A day is 24 hours. From the time you wake up one morning to the time you wake up the next morning is one day.

Circle the amount of time each event would take.

brushing teeth

minutes   hours

going to school

minutes   hours

playing soccer

days   hours

vacation

minutes   days

card game

seconds   minutes

blowing a bubble

minutes   seconds

Note: Have children do something for a second, a minute, and an hour.

Elapsed Time

Elapsed time is the time that has passed.

If you start dinner at

and finish at

then 30 minutes have passed.

If you start playing at

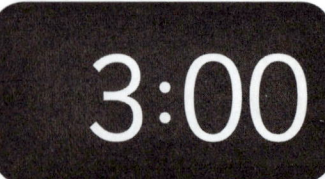

and finish at

then you played for 2 hours.

You walk the dog at `10:30`

and come home at `11:00`

You were walking for ____ minutes/ hours/ days

You fall asleep at `4:00`

and wake up at `6:00`

You were asleep for ____ minutes/ hours/ days.

Clare goes to Sarah's house at

She stays for 3 hours.

Clare left Sarah's house at ____ o'clock.

Note: Practice finding elapsed time with children as they do normal activities.

AM and PM

At 8 o'clock, it could be morning or night.
At 12:00, it could be noon or midnight.

You use AM and PM to help tell time.

AM is between midnight and noon.
Night time ends and day time starts in AM.

PM is between noon and midnight.
Morning ends and night time starts in PM.

Look at the digital clock.

7:00 AM

It shows you that it is AM. It is 7 o'clock in the morning.

7:00 PM

It shows you that it is PM. It is 7 o'clock in the evening.

What time do you think each of these things happen? Write AM or PM next to each picture.

Note: Throughout the day, ask children if the current time is AM or PM.

17

Using the Calendar

A calendar tells you about time, too.

Here are two months. There are 12 months in a year.

June

Mon	Tue	Wed	Thu	Fri	Sat	Sun
	1	2	3	4	5	6
7	8	9	10	11	12	13
14	15	16	17	18	19	20
21	22	23	24	25	26	27
28	29	30				

Each small square is a day.

Each row is a week.

July

Mon	Tue	Wed	Thu	Fri	Sat	Sun
			1	2	3	4
5	6	7	8	9	10	11
12	13	14	15	16	17	18
19	20	21	22	23	24	25
26	27	28	29	30	31	

Each big square is a month.

18

How many Mondays are in June?   ___

How many Saturdays are in July?   ___

How many Wednesdays are in July?   ___

Which month has more
Fridays, June or July?   ___ ___ ___ ___

What day of the week is July 10?

___ ___ ___ ___ ___ ___ ___

What day of the week is June 1?

___ ___ ___ ___ ___ ___

Note: Let children help you mark important dates on the calendar, such as birthdays.

19

Coins

Coins are made of metal. Each kind of coin has its own name. Each kind of coin also has its own value.

This is a penny.
A penny is 1 cent, or 1¢.

This is a nickel.
A nickel is 5 cents, or 5¢.

This is a dime.
A dime is 10 cents, or 10¢.

This is a quarter.
A quarter is 25 cents, or 25¢.

Draw a line to match the front and back of each coin.

Write the value of each coin.

_____

_____

_____

_____

Note: Children can use real coins to practice naming coins and their values.

Bills

Bills are made of paper. Each kind of bill has its own name and value.

This is a $1 bill.

A $1 bill is 1 dollar. It is worth 100 pennies.

This is a $5 bill.

A $5 bill is 5 dollars. It is worth five $1 bills.

This is a $10 bill.

A $10 bill is 10 dollars. It is worth ten $1 bills or two $5 bills.

This is a $20 bill.

A $20 bill is 20 dollars. It is worth 20 $1 bills, four $5 bills, or two $10 bills.

Draw a line to match the front and back of each bill.

Circle the correct value of each bill.

 $5
                       $1

 $10
                       $5

 $1
                       $10

 $10
                       $20

 $10
                       $5

 $50
                       $20

 $20
                       $5

 $1
                       $20

Note: Show children where to find the value on a bill.

Counting Coins

When you have a group of coins, you can count them to see how much money you have.

Look at these coins:

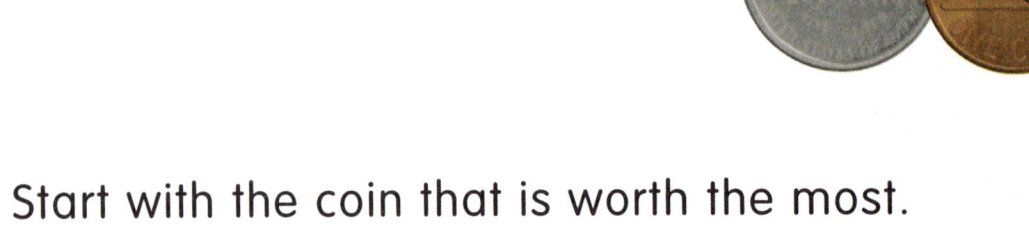

Start with the coin that is worth the most. The quarter is 25 cents.

Now count the dimes. Start at 25 cents because that's what you counted already. 25¢ + 10¢ + 10¢ = 45¢.

Now add on the nickel. Start at 45 cents. 45¢ + 5¢ = 50¢.

Finally add the pennies. Start at 50 cents. 50¢ + 1¢ + 1¢ + 1¢ + 1¢ = 54¢.

Look at each group of coins and count how much money there is.

_____

_____

_____

_____

Note: Encourage children to place a dot on each coin to help them count.

Equal Amounts

Different types of money can add up to the same amount.

Look at these two groups of money.

There is $20 in each group. The two groups are equal.

Now look at the next two groups of money.

There is 25¢ in each group. The two groups are equal.

Draw a line to match the groups that have the same amount of money.

Note: First, children could count the value of each group of money and write it down.

27

Comparing

Sometimes two groups of money are not the same.

Look at these two groups of money.

The money on the left is $10. The money on the right is $9.
$10 is greater than $9.

Now look at the next two groups of money.

The money on the left is 30¢. The money on the right is 11¢.
11¢ is less than 30¢.

Compare the groups of money.
Write > for "greater than"
or < for "less than."

 _____

 _____

 _____

 _____

 _____

Note: The point of > or < is always pointing to the smaller value.

Do you have Enough?

Counting and comparing money helps you shop. If you have more money or the exact money, then you have enough to buy what you want.

Look at the price of the ball.

75¢

Now count the money.

You have 100¢ or $1. This is more than the price of the ball. You can buy the ball.

Look at the price of the doll.

Count the money.

$7

You have $6. This is less than the price of the doll. You do not have enough money to buy the doll.

Look at the price and count the money.
Is there enough money? Add a check for
yes and a cross for no.

☐ 25¢

☐ 60¢

☐ $6

☐ 80¢

☐ $5

Note: If children have more than the price, they have enough money.

31

Notes for Parents and Teachers

- Get a toy clock, or make one from cardboard. Let children move the hands of the clock to match a given time, or move the hands and let children name the time.

- Expose children to analog clocks with Arabic numbers, Roman numerals, and other styles of numbering.

- Relate the numbers on the clock to skip counting by 5 since each number represents 5 minutes.

- Give your child an analog watch. This will be great incentive to learn how to tell time!

- Children should understand that "o'clock" is only for time to the hour. Teach children phrases such as "half past," "minutes before," and "minutes after."

- Let children help you shop. They can find items of a certain price or count out money.

- Explain to children that the bank holds money for people. It does not give money away.

- Consider giving children an allowance. This gives them a chance to save and set goals for how to use the money.

- Make up rhymes about each coin to help children identify them. For example, "Penny, Penny simply spent, it is brown and worth 1 cent" will help children identify a penny and know the value.

- Many storybooks help explain time and money in a humorous and entertaining way. For example, books about a visit from the tooth fairy. Reading these with young children will help them understand the concepts of time and money better.